The Berry

M000074902

Story by Jan Anderson
Photography by Lindsay Edwards

Robbie Matt

![Rigby logo]
Rigby®
A Harcourt Achieve Imprint

www.Rigby.com
1-800-531-5015

"Mom is going to be home late from work today," said Dad.

"Let's make her a cake," said Matt.

"Yes," said Robbie, "we can have it after dinner."

The boys helped Dad.

"Mom will love this cake,"
said Matt.

"We will, too," laughed Robbie.

"You can go outside and play now,"
said Dad.
"The cake will take a long time
to bake."

Matt and Robbie went outside
to play.

"Matt! Robbie!" shouted Dad.

"The cake is done.

Come and see it."

The boys ran back inside.

"It smells good," said Robbie.

"Yes," said Matt,
"but look at it.
The top is going down!"

The top of the cake
slowly went down.

"It's not looking very good,
is it?" laughed Dad.

"Mom will not like a cake
that looks like this," said Matt.

"We can make the cake look better
with some berries," said Robbie.
"They can go on the top
like this."

"Quick!" said Matt.
"Here comes Mom!"

"Who made this beautiful cake?"
said Mom.

"We did!" laughed Matt and Robbie.